The Ultimate Guide to Earning Money Online

By: Gene Naro Geneta

Chapter 1: Introduction to Online Money-Making

Understanding the Digital Landscape:

The digital landscape refers to the vast and dynamic world of the internet where opportunities for earning money online abound. It encompasses various platforms, technologies, and trends that shape the way individuals and businesses interact, create value, and generate income. Understanding the digital landscape involves familiarizing oneself with the different online money-making avenues such as freelancing, e-commerce, affiliate marketing, blogging, and more. It also requires staying updated on the latest digital tools, strategies, and market trends to leverage opportunities effectively.

Benefits of Earning Money Online:

Earning money online offers numerous benefits that make it an attractive option for many individuals. Some of the key benefits include:

1. Flexibility: Online money-making allows for flexible work hours and the ability to work from anywhere with an internet connection.
2. Diverse Income Streams: Online platforms offer a wide range of opportunities to earn money through various channels such as freelancing, e-commerce, and passive income streams.
3. Low Start-up Costs: Many online business models have low entry barriers, making it accessible for individuals with limited capital to start their ventures.
4. Global Reach: The internet provides a global marketplace, allowing individuals to reach a wider audience and expand their earning potential.
5. Scalability: Online businesses can be scaled up quickly and efficiently, enabling rapid growth and increased profitability.

Common Misconceptions and Pitfalls:

While online money-making presents exciting opportunities, there are also common misconceptions and pitfalls that individuals should be aware of to navigate the digital landscape successfully. Some of these include:

1. Get-Rich-Quick Schemes: Beware of schemes promising overnight wealth without effort or investment. Building a sustainable online income requires time, effort, and dedication.
2. Lack of Discipline: Working online can be distracting, leading to procrastination and reduced productivity. Developing a disciplined work routine is essential for success.
3. Market Saturation: Some online niches may be oversaturated, making it challenging to stand out and succeed. Researching niche markets and finding unique value propositions is crucial.
4. Scams and Fraud: The online world is also rife with scams and fraudulent schemes. It's important to exercise caution, conduct due diligence, and verify the legitimacy of opportunities before committing.

Case Studies:

- Understanding the Digital Landscape: Case Study - Amazon's Dominance in E-commerce

Amazon's success story exemplifies the power of understanding the digital landscape. By recognizing the potential of e-commerce early on and leveraging technology to streamline operations and enhance customer experience, Amazon has become a global giant in online retail.

- Benefits of Earning Money Online: Case Study - Pat Flynn's Passive Income Success

Pat Flynn, a renowned online entrepreneur, has built a successful online business by diversifying his income streams through blogging, podcasting, and affiliate marketing. His story highlights the benefits of earning money online, including flexibility, scalability, and the ability to generate passive income.

- Common Misconceptions and Pitfalls: Case Study - Cryptocurrency Scams

The rise of cryptocurrency has attracted scammers looking to exploit individuals seeking quick profits. Numerous cases of fraudulent ICOs, Ponzi schemes, and phishing scams underscore the importance of being cautious and conducting thorough research before investing in online opportunities.

Chapter 2: Setting the Foundation

Identifying Your Skills and Interests:

Identifying your skills and interests is a crucial first step in setting the foundation for earning money online. By recognizing what you excel at and what you are passionate about, you can align your online endeavors with your strengths and preferences. Conducting a skills assessment and self-reflection can help you pinpoint areas where you can add value and derive satisfaction. Whether it's writing, graphic design, programming, teaching, or any other skill, leveraging your expertise and interests can lead to a more fulfilling and successful online venture.

Goal Setting and Financial Planning:

Goal setting and financial planning are essential components of building a sustainable online income stream. Setting clear, measurable goals helps provide direction and motivation for your online activities. Whether your goal is to earn a certain amount of money per month, launch a successful e-commerce store, or achieve financial independence, outlining specific objectives and creating a roadmap to achieve them is key. Financial planning involves budgeting, saving, investing, and managing expenses to ensure that your online earnings contribute to your long-term financial stability and growth.

Creating a Conducive Work Environment:

Creating a conducive work environment is vital for productivity, focus, and overall well-being when earning money online. Your work environment should be tailored to suit your work style and preferences, whether it's a home office, a co-working space, or a coffee shop. Factors such as lighting, ergonomics, organization, and minimal distractions play a role in optimizing your work environment. Establishing boundaries, setting work hours, and eliminating distractions can help you maintain a healthy work-life balance and maximize your online earning potential.

Case Studies:

- Identifying Your Skills and Interests: Case Study - Michelle Phan's Beauty Empire

Michelle Phan, a beauty influencer and entrepreneur, identified her passion for makeup artistry and content creation early on. By leveraging her skills in makeup application and video production, she built a successful online brand through YouTube tutorials, social media presence, and her own cosmetics line. Michelle's story demonstrates the power of aligning skills and interests with online opportunities.

- Goal Setting and Financial Planning: Case Study - Dave Ramsey's Financial Advice Platform

Dave Ramsey, a renowned financial expert, established a successful online platform focused on personal finance education and coaching. Through goal setting, budgeting tools, and financial planning resources, Dave has helped millions of individuals achieve financial freedom and stability. His platform exemplifies the importance of setting clear financial goals and planning for long-term success.

- Creating a Conducive Work Environment: Case Study - Remote Work at Buffer

Buffer, a social media management company, has embraced remote work and created a conducive virtual work environment for its employees. With flexible work hours, communication tools, and a supportive culture, Buffer has fostered a productive and collaborative remote work environment. Their approach showcases how a well-designed work environment can enhance productivity and job satisfaction in the online realm.

Chapter 3: Freelancing

Overview of Freelancing Platforms:

Freelancing platforms serve as marketplaces where freelancers can connect with clients seeking their services. These platforms facilitate the exchange of skills, projects, and payments in a structured and secure environment. Popular freelancing platforms include Upwork, Freelancer, Fiverr, and Toptal, each offering a diverse range of job categories and opportunities for freelancers. Understanding the features, fees, and user guidelines of freelancing platforms is essential for freelancers to navigate the online marketplace effectively and find suitable projects.

Building a Strong Profile and Portfolio:

A strong profile and portfolio are essential for freelancers to showcase their skills, experience, and credibility to potential clients. A well-crafted profile should highlight your expertise, qualifications, past work samples, and client testimonials. Including a professional headshot, a compelling bio, and relevant keywords can improve visibility and attract clients. Building a portfolio of high-quality work samples, case studies, and testimonials demonstrates your capabilities and builds trust with clients, increasing your chances of securing freelance projects.

Finding and Securing Freelance Gigs:

Finding and securing freelance gigs requires proactive networking, effective communication, and a strategic approach to pitching your services. Freelancers can leverage various strategies to find gigs, such as browsing job listings on freelancing platforms, networking on social media and professional forums, reaching out to potential clients directly, and collaborating with other freelancers or agencies. Crafting personalized proposals, showcasing relevant experience, and demonstrating value to clients are key factors in securing freelance projects and building long-term relationships with clients.

Case Studies:

- Overview of Freelancing Platforms: Case Study - Upwork's Global Freelance Marketplace
Upwork is a leading freelancing platform that connects freelancers with clients worldwide. With a diverse range of job categories, secure payment systems, and robust project management tools, Upwork provides freelancers with access to a global marketplace of opportunities. Freelancers can leverage Upwork's platform to showcase their skills, bid on projects, and build successful freelance careers.
- Building a Strong Profile and Portfolio: Case Study - Graphic Designer Sarah's Portfolio Success
Sarah, a freelance graphic designer, built a strong online portfolio showcasing her design projects, client testimonials, and creative process. By curating a visually appealing portfolio website, optimizing her profile on freelancing platforms, and regularly updating her portfolio with new work, Sarah attracted high-quality clients and secured lucrative design projects. Her success highlights the importance of a strong portfolio in establishing credibility and winning freelance gigs.

- Finding and Securing Freelance Gigs: Case Study - Content Writer John's Networking Strategy

John, a freelance content writer, utilized a proactive networking strategy to find and secure freelance gigs. By engaging with industry professionals on LinkedIn, attending virtual networking events, and reaching out to potential clients via email, John established valuable connections and landed recurring writing projects. His strategic networking approach demonstrates the effectiveness of building relationships and actively seeking freelance opportunities in the online marketplace.

Chapter 4: Online Surveys and Market Research

Participating in Paid Surveys:

Participating in paid surveys is a popular way to earn money online by sharing your opinions and feedback on various products, services, and brands. Companies and market research firms conduct online surveys to gather consumer insights, and they compensate participants for their time and input. Paid survey opportunities can be found on dedicated survey websites, survey panels, and through market research companies. By signing up for reputable survey platforms, completing surveys consistently, and providing honest feedback, individuals can earn rewards such as cash, gift cards, or prizes for their participation.

Joining Market Research Panels:

Joining market research panels involves becoming a part of a group of individuals who are willing to provide feedback and opinions on products, services, or concepts. Market research panels are often used by companies to conduct in-depth studies, focus groups, and product testing to gather valuable insights from consumers. By joining market research panels, participants can contribute to shaping products and services, influencing marketing strategies, and earning rewards for their valuable feedback. Panelists may receive invitations to participate in surveys, interviews, or product trials based on their demographics and interests.

Maximizing Earnings from Surveys:

Maximizing earnings from surveys involves adopting strategies to increase the efficiency and profitability of participating in online surveys and market research activities. Some tips for maximizing earnings include:

- Signing up for multiple survey platforms to access a variety of survey opportunities.
- Completing profile surveys to receive more targeted survey invitations.
- Setting aside dedicated time for taking surveys regularly to increase earnings.
- Participating in high-paying surveys, focus groups, or product testing opportunities.
- Redeeming rewards promptly and exploring bonus incentives offered by survey platforms.
- Providing thoughtful and detailed responses to survey questions to qualify for more surveys and earn higher rewards.

Case Studies:

- Participating in Paid Surveys: Case Study - Survey Junkie's User Success

Survey Junkie is a popular paid survey platform that rewards users for sharing their opinions on various topics. Users like Sarah, who dedicated time to completing surveys consistently, earned significant rewards in the form of cash and gift cards. By providing detailed feedback and participating in surveys regularly, Sarah maximized her earnings on Survey Junkie and enjoyed a steady stream of rewards for her participation.

- Joining Market Research Panels: Case Study - Nielsen Consumer Panel Insights

Nielsen Consumer Panel is a renowned market research panel that gathers consumer data to inform industry trends and consumer behavior. Panelists like John, who joined the Nielsen Consumer Panel, contributed valuable insights through surveys, product scanning, and feedback. By actively participating in market research activities, John not only earned rewards but also influenced product development and marketing strategies through his feedback.

- Maximizing Earnings from Surveys: Case Study - Maximizing Survey Rewards with Swagbucks

Swagbucks is a popular rewards platform that offers paid surveys, tasks, and other earning opportunities. Users like Emily maximized their earnings on Swagbucks by diversifying their activities, completing surveys daily, and taking advantage of bonus incentives. By staying engaged with the platform, exploring various earning options, and redeeming rewards efficiently, Emily significantly increased her earnings from online surveys and tasks.

Chapter 5: E-commerce and Dropshipping

Setting Up an Online Store:

Setting up an online store is a fundamental step in establishing an e-commerce business and selling products or services online. Key aspects of setting up an online store include:

- Choosing a platform: Selecting an e-commerce platform such as Shopify, WooCommerce, or BigCommerce to create and manage your online store.
- Designing the store: Customizing the store layout, branding, and product displays to create a visually appealing and user-friendly shopping experience.

- Adding products: Uploading product listings, images, descriptions, and pricing to showcase your offerings and attract customers.
- Setting up payment and shipping: Integrating secure payment gateways, setting up shipping options, and configuring tax settings to enable smooth transactions.

Dropshipping Business Model:

Dropshipping is a popular e-commerce business model where the seller does not hold inventory but fulfills orders by purchasing products from a third party and having them shipped directly to the customer. Key aspects of the dropshipping business model include:

- Selecting suppliers: Identifying reliable dropshipping suppliers or wholesalers to source products from and fulfill customer orders.
- Listing products: Adding dropshipped products to your online store and setting prices to cover costs and generate profits.

- Order fulfillment: Processing customer orders, forwarding them to the supplier for shipment, and managing customer inquiries and returns.
- Profit margins: Calculating profit margins by considering product costs, shipping fees, and other expenses to ensure profitability in dropshipping.

Marketing and Driving Traffic to Your Store:

Marketing plays a crucial role in driving traffic to your online store and attracting customers to make purchases. Strategies for marketing an e-commerce store include:

- Search engine optimization (SEO): Optimizing product descriptions, meta tags, and website content to improve visibility and ranking on search engines.
- Social media marketing: Leveraging social media platforms like Facebook, Instagram, and Pinterest to promote products, engage with customers, and drive traffic to the store.
- Paid advertising: Running online ads on platforms like Google Ads, Facebook Ads, and Instagram Ads to target specific audiences and increase store visibility.
- Content marketing: Creating valuable content such as blog posts, videos, and infographics to educate, inspire, and attract potential customers to the store.

Case Studies:

- Setting Up an Online Store: Case Study - Warby Parker's Online Eyewear Success
Warby Parker, an eyewear company, set up a successful online store that revolutionized the eyewear industry. By offering affordable, stylish glasses online and providing a seamless shopping experience, Warby Parker attracted a large customer base and disrupted traditional brick-and-mortar eyewear retail.
- Dropshipping Business Model: Case Study - Oberlo's Dropshipping Platform
Oberlo, a dropshipping platform integrated with Shopify, enables entrepreneurs to start dropshipping businesses with ease. By connecting sellers with suppliers and automating order fulfillment, Oberlo has empowered thousands of individuals to launch and scale profitable dropshipping ventures.
- Marketing and Driving Traffic to Your Store: Case Study - Glossier's Social Media Marketing Strategy
Glossier, a beauty brand, leveraged social media marketing to drive traffic and sales to its online store. By cultivating a strong presence on Instagram, engaging with followers, and creating user-generated content, Glossier built a loyal community of customers who actively promoted and purchased products from the brand's online store.

Chapter 6: Affiliate Marketing

Understanding Affiliate Marketing:

Affiliate marketing is a performance-based marketing strategy where affiliates earn a commission for promoting products or services of other companies. Key aspects of affiliate marketing include:

- Affiliate relationships: Affiliates partner with merchants or advertisers to promote their products through unique tracking links.
- Commission structure: Affiliates earn commissions based on predefined actions, such as sales, leads, clicks, or sign-ups generated through their referral links.
- Tracking and analytics: Affiliate networks or platforms track affiliate activities, conversions, and commissions to provide performance insights.

- Compliance and disclosure: Affiliates are required to disclose their affiliate relationships and adhere to ethical marketing practices to maintain credibility and trust with their audience.

Choosing the Right Affiliate Programs:

Choosing the right affiliate programs is essential for success in affiliate marketing. Considerations for selecting affiliate programs include:

- Relevance: Choose affiliate programs that align with your niche, audience interests, and content to ensure relevance and engagement.
- Commission structure: Evaluate commission rates, payment terms, and cookie durations to maximize earnings and profitability.
- Product quality: Partner with reputable merchants offering high-quality products or services that resonate with your audience and reflect positively on your brand.
- Support and resources: Look for affiliate programs that provide marketing materials, tracking tools, and support to help affiliates succeed in promoting their offers.

Strategies for Successful Affiliate Marketing:

Implementing effective strategies is key to achieving success in affiliate marketing. Strategies for successful affiliate marketing include:

- Content creation: Produce high-quality, valuable content such as reviews, tutorials, and recommendations to educate and persuade your audience to make purchase decisions.
- Audience targeting: Understand your audience's needs, preferences, and pain points to tailor your affiliate promotions and recommendations for maximum relevance and impact.
- Diversification: Promote a mix of affiliate products, services, and programs to diversify revenue streams and reduce dependency on a single affiliate partner.
- Relationship building: Cultivate relationships with merchants, affiliate managers, and fellow affiliates to collaborate, exchange insights, and access exclusive opportunities for growth and optimization.

Case Studies:

- Understanding Affiliate Marketing: Case Study - Amazon Associates Program

Amazon Associates is one of the largest affiliate marketing programs, allowing affiliates to earn commissions by promoting Amazon products. Affiliates like Sarah leverage Amazon's vast product selection, reliable tracking system, and competitive commissions to monetize their websites and earn passive income through affiliate marketing.

- Choosing the Right Affiliate Programs: Case Study - ShareASale Affiliate Network

ShareASale is a reputable affiliate network that connects affiliates with a wide range of merchants and affiliate programs across various industries. Affiliates like John benefit from ShareASale's diverse program offerings, competitive commissions, and user-friendly platform to find and join affiliate programs that align with their niche and audience.

- Strategies for Successful Affiliate Marketing: Case Study - Pat Flynn's Affiliate Marketing Success

Pat Flynn, a renowned affiliate marketer and entrepreneur, has built a successful affiliate marketing business by implementing strategies such as transparent disclosure, authentic recommendations, and value-driven content. Through his platform, Smart Passive Income, Pat has cultivated trust with his audience, generated significant affiliate revenue, and established himself as a trusted authority in the affiliate marketing space.

Chapter 7: Blogging and Content Creation

Starting a Blog:

Starting a blog is a creative and rewarding endeavor that allows individuals to share their thoughts, expertise, and experiences with a global audience. Key steps in starting a blog include:

- Choosing a niche: Select a specific topic or niche that interests you and aligns with your expertise and passion.
- Selecting a platform: Decide on a blogging platform such as WordPress, Blogger, or Medium to create and manage your blog.
- Creating content: Begin writing and publishing blog posts that provide value, insights, information, or entertainment to your target audience.
- Designing the blog: Customize the blog's layout, theme, colors, and branding to create a visually appealing and cohesive online presence.

Monetizing Your Blog Through Ads and Sponsored Content:

Monetizing a blog involves generating income from various sources, such as advertisements and sponsored content. Strategies for monetizing your blog include:

- Display ads: Implementing display advertising networks like Google AdSense to display relevant ads on your blog and earn revenue based on ad clicks or impressions.
- Sponsored content: Collaborating with brands or advertisers to create sponsored posts, reviews, or endorsements that promote their products or services in exchange for compensation.
- Affiliate marketing: Incorporating affiliate links and promotions in your blog posts to earn commissions for driving sales or leads to affiliate partners.
- Premium content: Offering premium content, courses, or memberships to your audience for a fee to provide exclusive value and generate recurring revenue.

Building a Loyal Audience:

Building a loyal audience is essential for the long-term success and sustainability of a blog. Strategies for building a loyal audience include:

- Consistent content creation: Regularly publishing high-quality, engaging, and valuable content to keep your audience informed and entertained.
- Engagement and interaction: Interacting with your audience through comments, social media, email newsletters, and live events to foster a sense of community and connection.
- Personal branding: Establishing a strong personal brand, voice, and identity that resonates with your audience and distinguishes your blog from competitors.
- Providing value: Addressing audience needs, solving problems, answering questions, and delivering relevant and useful content that adds value to your readers' lives.

Case Studies:

- Starting a Blog: Case Study - The Minimalists' Blogging Success
The Minimalists, Joshua Fields Millburn and Ryan Nicodemus, started a blog focused on minimalism, simplicity, and intentional living. By sharing their personal stories, insights, and practical tips on their blog, they attracted a loyal following and built a thriving online community around their minimalist lifestyle philosophy.
- Monetizing Your Blog Through Ads and Sponsored Content: Case Study - Cupcakes and Cashmere's Sponsored Content Strategy

Emily Schuman, the creator of Cupcakes and Cashmere, monetizes her lifestyle blog through sponsored content partnerships with fashion, beauty, and lifestyle brands. By integrating sponsored posts seamlessly into her content, Emily maintains authenticity and relevance while earning income from brand collaborations.

- Building a Loyal Audience: Case Study - Neil Patel's Audience Engagement Tactics

Neil Patel, a renowned digital marketer and blogger, has built a loyal audience through consistent content creation, in-depth guides, and interactive tools on his blog. By engaging with his audience through comments, social media, and webinars, Neil has cultivated a dedicated following of marketers and entrepreneurs who value his expertise and insights.

Chapter 8: Online Tutoring and Courses

Offering Online Tutoring Services:

Offering online tutoring services provides an opportunity to share knowledge, help others learn, and earn income through virtual teaching sessions. Key aspects of offering online tutoring services include:

- Subject expertise: Identify your areas of expertise and the subjects or topics you are passionate about teaching.
- Virtual platforms: Choose online tutoring platforms or tools such as Zoom, Skype, or specialized tutoring websites to conduct virtual tutoring sessions.
- Lesson planning: Prepare lesson plans, materials, and resources tailored to the needs and learning styles of your students.
- Communication and feedback: Maintain clear communication with students, provide feedback on their progress, and offer support to enhance their learning experience.

Creating and Selling Online Courses:

Creating and selling online courses is a popular way to share knowledge, skills, and expertise with a broader audience and generate passive income. Strategies for creating and selling online courses include:

- Course topic selection: Choose a relevant and in-demand course topic that aligns with your expertise and addresses a specific need or problem.
- Course creation: Develop course content, modules, videos, quizzes, and assignments to deliver a comprehensive and engaging learning experience.
- Platform selection: Select an online course platform such as Udemy, Teachable, or Coursera to host and sell your courses to a global audience.
- Marketing and promotion: Promote your online courses through social media, email marketing, partnerships, and advertising to attract students and drive course sales.

Platforms for Teaching and Learning:

Platforms for teaching and learning provide a digital infrastructure for educators and students to engage in online education. Popular platforms for teaching and learning include:

- Udemy: An online course marketplace where instructors can create and sell courses on a wide range of topics.
- Coursera: An e-learning platform offering courses, certificates, and degree programs from universities and institutions worldwide.
- Khan Academy: A non-profit educational platform providing free educational resources, tutorials, and practice exercises across various subjects.
- Skillshare: An online learning community where creators can offer classes on creative skills, design, business, and more to a global audience.

Case Studies:

- Offering Online Tutoring Services: Case Study - Varsity Tutors' Virtual Tutoring Success

Varsity Tutors is a leading online tutoring platform that connects students with expert tutors for personalized virtual tutoring sessions. Tutors like Sarah leverage Varsity Tutors' platform to offer one-on-one tutoring in subjects such as math, science, and languages, helping students achieve academic success and mastery in their studies.

- Creating and Selling Online Courses: Case Study - MasterClass's Celebrity-Led Courses
MasterClass is an online education platform that offers celebrity-led courses in various fields such as music, writing, cooking, and entrepreneurship. Renowned experts like Gordon Ramsay, Margaret Atwood, and Serena Williams create and sell online courses on MasterClass, providing students with exclusive access to their expertise and insights.
- Platforms for Teaching and Learning: Case Study - Udemy's Global Course Marketplace
Udemy is a popular online course marketplace where instructors can create, publish, and sell courses to a global audience. Instructors like John use Udemy's platform to teach courses on programming, digital marketing, and personal development, reaching students worldwide and earning income from course sales.

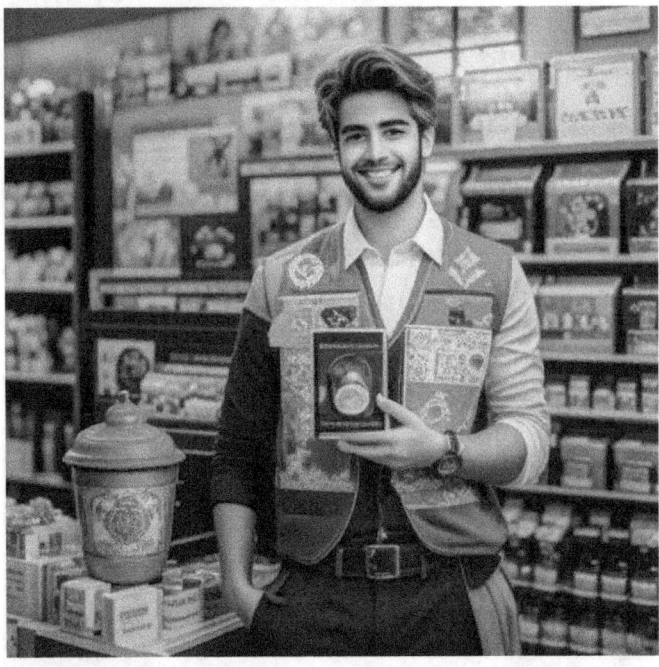

Chapter 9: Virtual Assistance and Remote Work

Providing Virtual Assistance Services:

Virtual assistance services involve providing administrative, creative, technical, or specialized support to clients remotely. Key aspects of providing virtual assistance services include:

- Skillset: Identify your skills, strengths, and areas of expertise that align with the services you can offer as a virtual assistant.
- Services offered: Determine the services you will provide, such as email management, social media management, data entry, customer support, or project coordination.
- Communication tools: Utilize communication tools like email, messaging apps, project management platforms, and video conferencing to collaborate with clients effectively.
- Professionalism: Maintain professionalism, confidentiality, and reliability in delivering high-quality virtual assistance services to clients.

Finding Remote Work Opportunities:

Finding remote work opportunities allows individuals to work from anywhere and access a variety of job roles and industries. Strategies for finding remote work opportunities include:

- Remote job boards: Explore remote job boards such as Remote.co, FlexJobs, We Work Remotely, and Remote OK to discover remote job listings across different sectors.
- Networking: Build professional connections, attend virtual networking events, and engage with remote work communities to access hidden job opportunities and referrals.
- Freelancing platforms: Join freelancing platforms like Upwork, Freelancer, and Fiverr to find remote projects, gigs, and clients seeking virtual assistance and remote services.
- Industry-specific websites: Visit industry-specific websites, forums, and job portals related to your expertise or field to find remote job openings tailored to your skills and interests.

Managing Time and Tasks Effectively:

Managing time and tasks effectively is essential for remote workers and virtual assistants to maintain productivity and meet deadlines. Strategies for managing time and tasks effectively include:

- Time management tools: Use productivity tools like Trello, Asana, Todoist, or Google Calendar to organize tasks, set priorities, and track progress on projects.
- Time blocking: Allocate dedicated time blocks for specific tasks, projects, and activities to focus on one task at a time and avoid multitasking.
- Communication boundaries: Establish clear communication boundaries with clients, colleagues, and team members to set expectations, availability, and response times.
- Self-care and breaks: Prioritize self-care, take regular breaks, and practice mindfulness to avoid burnout, maintain work-life balance, and recharge for optimal performance.

Case Studies:

- Providing Virtual Assistance Services: Case Study - Time Etc's Virtual Assistant Success

Time Etc is a virtual assistant company that matches skilled assistants with clients needing support. Virtual assistants like Sarah provide services such as scheduling, email management, research, and project coordination, helping clients streamline their tasks and focus on their core responsibilities.

- Finding Remote Work Opportunities: Case Study - Remote Developer John's Job Search Success

John, a remote developer, found remote work opportunities through networking on LinkedIn, applying to remote job postings on platforms like Remote.co, and showcasing his portfolio on GitHub. By actively seeking remote work opportunities and engaging with remote work communities, John secured remote projects and freelance gigs aligned with his programming skills.

- Managing Time and Tasks Effectively: Case Study - Virtual Assistant Emily's Time Management Strategies

Emily, a virtual assistant, uses time management tools like Trello and Google Calendar to organize tasks, set deadlines, and track client projects. By implementing time blocking, prioritizing tasks, and establishing communication boundaries with clients, Emily effectively manages her time, delivers quality work, and maintains a healthy work-life balance as a virtual assistant.

Chapter 10: Investing and Trading Online

Introduction to Online Investing:

Online investing refers to the process of buying and selling financial assets, such as stocks, bonds, mutual funds, and cryptocurrencies, through online platforms. Key aspects of online investing include:

- Investment goals: Define your investment objectives, whether it's wealth accumulation, retirement planning, passive income generation, or capital appreciation.
- Investment horizon: Determine your investment time horizon, whether you are a short-term trader or a long-term investor looking to build wealth over time.
- Risk tolerance: Assess your risk tolerance and comfort level with market volatility, uncertainty, and potential losses when making investment decisions.
- Diversification: Implement a diversified investment strategy by spreading your investments across different asset classes, sectors, and geographic regions to reduce risk and maximize returns.

Trading Stocks, Cryptocurrencies, and Forex:

Trading stocks, cryptocurrencies, and forex are common forms of online trading that involve buying and selling financial instruments for profit. Strategies for trading stocks, cryptocurrencies, and forex include:

- Stock trading: Buy and sell shares of publicly traded companies on stock exchanges like NYSE or NASDAQ based on fundamental analysis, technical analysis, or market trends.
- Cryptocurrency trading: Trade digital currencies like Bitcoin, Ethereum, and Litecoin on cryptocurrency exchanges using technical analysis, market sentiment, and news events to make trading decisions.
- Forex trading: Trade currency pairs in the foreign exchange market based on economic indicators, geopolitical events, and technical analysis to speculate on currency price movements and profit from exchange rate fluctuations.

Risk Management and Strategies for Success:

Risk management and strategies for success are essential components of online investing and trading to protect capital and achieve investment goals. Strategies for risk management and success include:

- Stop-loss orders: Set stop-loss orders to limit potential losses and automatically sell investments if prices reach predetermined levels to manage risk.
- Position sizing: Determine appropriate position sizes based on risk tolerance, account size, and investment objectives to control risk exposure and avoid overleveraging.
- Research and analysis: Conduct thorough research, analysis, and due diligence on investments, markets, and trading opportunities to make informed decisions and minimize risks.

- Portfolio rebalancing: Regularly review and rebalance your investment portfolio by adjusting asset allocations, reallocating capital, and diversifying holdings to optimize returns and manage risk effectively.

Case Studies:

- Introduction to Online Investing: Case Study - Robo-Advisor Wealthfront's Automated Investing
Wealthfront is a robo-advisor platform that offers automated online investing services based on clients' risk tolerance, goals, and time horizon. Clients like Sarah benefit from Wealthfront's algorithmic investment approach, low fees, and diversified portfolios to achieve long-term investment growth and wealth accumulation.
- Trading Stocks, Cryptocurrencies, and Forex: Case Study - Crypto Trader John's Bitcoin Trading Success
John, a cryptocurrency trader, implements technical analysis, market research, and risk management strategies to trade Bitcoin and other cryptocurrencies profitably. By analyzing price charts, monitoring market trends, and applying risk management principles, John navigates the volatile cryptocurrency market and achieves trading success.
- Risk Management and Strategies for Success: Case Study - Stock Investor Emily's Portfolio Management
Emily, a stock investor, practices risk management by diversifying her stock portfolio, setting stop-loss orders, and conducting fundamental analysis on companies before investing. By following a disciplined investment approach, managing risk exposure, and staying informed about market trends, Emily achieves long-term success in online investing and stock trading.

Chapter 11: Passive Income Streams

Creating Passive Income Streams Online:

Creating passive income streams online involves generating income with minimal ongoing effort or time investment. Key aspects of creating passive income streams online include:

- Passive income sources: Identify passive income opportunities such as affiliate marketing, e-books, online courses, digital products, membership sites, and advertising revenue.
- Automation: Implement automation tools, systems, and processes to streamline passive income streams and reduce the need for constant supervision or active involvement.

- Scalability: Focus on scalable passive income sources that have the potential to grow and generate recurring income over time without significant additional effort.
- Monetization strategies: Explore different monetization strategies such as subscription models, affiliate partnerships, sponsored content, and digital product sales to diversify passive income streams.

Real Estate Crowdfunding and Investments:

Real estate crowdfunding and investments offer opportunities to invest in real estate projects, properties, or funds through online platforms. Strategies for real estate crowdfunding and investments include:

- Crowdfunding platforms: Participate in real estate crowdfunding platforms like Fundrise, RealtyMogul, or Crowdstreet to invest in commercial or residential properties, development projects, or real estate debt.

- Diversification: Diversify real estate investments across different properties, locations, and asset classes to reduce risk and maximize returns in a real estate portfolio.
- Due diligence: Conduct thorough due diligence, research, and analysis on real estate opportunities, market trends, property valuations, and investment risks before committing capital to real estate investments.
- Passive income potential: Evaluate the passive income potential of real estate investments through rental income, property appreciation, dividends, or distributions from real estate investment trusts (REITs) to generate passive cash flow.

Building a Portfolio of Passive Income Sources:

Building a portfolio of passive income sources involves diversifying income streams, investments, and revenue sources to create a stable and sustainable passive income stream. Strategies for building a portfolio of passive income sources include:

- Income diversification: Invest in a mix of passive income sources such as stocks, bonds, real estate, dividends, royalties, and online businesses to spread risk and maximize income potential.
- Risk management: Manage risk exposure, volatility, and market fluctuations by diversifying passive income sources, setting investment goals, and implementing risk management strategies to protect capital.
- Long-term perspective: Adopt a long-term investment approach, focus on building a diversified portfolio of passive income sources, and reinvest earnings to compound wealth and achieve financial independence over time.
- Passive income reinvestment: Reinvest passive income earnings into additional income-generating assets, investments, or business ventures to accelerate wealth accumulation, grow passive income streams, and achieve financial goals.

Case Studies:

- Creating Passive Income Streams Online: Case Study - Passive Income Blogger Sarah's Affiliate Marketing Success
Sarah, a passive income blogger, generates passive income online through affiliate marketing, sponsored content, and digital product sales on her blog. By creating valuable content, promoting affiliate products, and diversifying income streams, Sarah builds a sustainable passive income stream that generates revenue while she focuses on other projects and activities.
- Real Estate Crowdfunding and Investments: Case Study - Real Estate Investor John's Crowdfunding Portfolio

John, a real estate investor, diversifies his real estate portfolio through crowdfunding platforms like RealtyMogul and Fundrise. By investing in commercial properties, residential projects, and real estate funds, John earns passive income through rental yields, property appreciation, and real estate dividends, building a diversified real estate investment portfolio.

- Building a Portfolio of Passive Income Sources: Case Study - Passive Income Entrepreneur Emily's Diversified Portfolio

Emily, a passive income entrepreneur, builds a diversified portfolio of passive income sources that includes dividend stocks, rental properties, affiliate marketing, and online courses. By reinvesting passive income earnings, diversifying income streams, and focusing on long-term wealth building, Emily creates a resilient portfolio of passive income sources that generates sustainable cash flow and financial stability.

Chapter 12: Scaling and Diversifying Your Online Income

Scaling Your Online Business:

Scaling your online business involves expanding operations, increasing revenue, and growing your customer base to achieve sustainable growth. Key aspects of scaling your online business include:

- Scalability: Evaluate the scalability of your business model, products, services, and operations to accommodate growth and handle increased demand.
- Automation: Implement automation tools, processes, and systems to streamline workflows, improve efficiency, and reduce manual tasks as your business scales.
- Market expansion: Explore new markets, target audiences, product lines, or geographic regions to diversify revenue streams and reach a broader customer base.
- Customer retention: Focus on customer satisfaction, loyalty programs, and personalized experiences to retain existing customers, attract repeat business, and drive long-term growth.

Diversifying Income Streams:

Diversifying income streams involves generating revenue from multiple sources to reduce risk, increase income stability, and create a resilient financial portfolio. Strategies for diversifying income streams include:

- Multiple revenue streams: Develop and monetize multiple income streams such as affiliate marketing, e-commerce sales, online courses, rental properties, and freelance services to create a diversified income portfolio.
- Passive income sources: Invest in passive income opportunities like dividends, royalties, real estate investments, and automated online businesses to generate recurring income with minimal ongoing effort.
- Risk management: Spread income sources across different asset classes, industries, and markets to hedge against economic fluctuations, market volatility, and industry-specific risks that may impact individual income streams.
- Growth opportunities: Explore new income-generating ventures, partnerships, collaborations, and revenue models to expand your income streams, optimize earnings, and capitalize on emerging trends and opportunities.

Long-Term Sustainability and Growth:

Long-term sustainability and growth are essential for building a resilient and successful online income portfolio. Strategies for long-term sustainability and growth include:

- Strategic planning: Develop a long-term business strategy, set clear goals, and create a roadmap for sustainable growth, profitability, and market expansion.
- Continuous learning: Stay informed about industry trends, market developments, and technological advancements to adapt, innovate, and evolve your online business for long-term success.
- Financial management: Monitor cash flow, expenses, and profitability, and make informed financial decisions to ensure financial stability, reinvest profits, and fuel growth initiatives.
- Adaptability: Be flexible, agile, and responsive to changes, challenges, and opportunities in the online marketplace to pivot, adjust strategies, and capitalize on evolving consumer behaviors and market dynamics.

Case Studies:

- Scaling Your Online Business: Case Study - E-commerce Entrepreneur Sarah's Growth Strategy

Sarah, an e-commerce entrepreneur, scales her online business by expanding product lines, optimizing marketing campaigns, and enhancing customer service. By investing in technology, hiring additional staff, and diversifying product offerings, Sarah achieves exponential growth, increases sales revenue, and establishes a strong brand presence in the competitive e-commerce market.

- Diversifying Income Streams: Case Study - Passive Income Investor John's Diversified Portfolio

John, a passive income investor, diversifies his income streams by investing in dividend stocks, rental properties, affiliate marketing, and online courses. By creating a diversified income portfolio with multiple revenue sources, John minimizes risk, maximizes income potential, and achieves financial stability and growth over the long term.

- Long-Term Sustainability and Growth: Case Study - Digital Marketing Agency Emily's Sustainable Growth Plan

Emily, the founder of a digital marketing agency, focuses on long-term sustainability and growth by investing in employee training, client relationships, and technology upgrades. By fostering a culture of innovation, delivering exceptional service, and adapting to industry changes, Emily's agency achieves sustainable growth, client retention, and industry leadership in the competitive digital marketing landscape.

Chapter 13: Overcoming Challenges and Staying Motivated

Dealing with Setbacks and Failures:

Dealing with setbacks and failures is an inevitable part of any journey, including building an online income stream. Key aspects of handling setbacks and failures include:

- Resilience: Cultivate resilience by viewing setbacks as learning opportunities, embracing challenges, and bouncing back stronger from failures.
- Reflection: Reflect on setbacks to identify lessons learned, areas for improvement, and strategies for overcoming obstacles in the future.
- Adaptability: Adapt to changing circumstances, pivot strategies, and adjust goals to navigate setbacks and setbacks effectively.
- Persistence: Maintain a positive mindset, stay persistent, and persevere through challenges to achieve long-term success and growth.

Maintaining Motivation and Focus:

Maintaining motivation and focus is essential for staying productive, achieving goals, and sustaining momentum in online income endeavors. Strategies for maintaining motivation and focus include:

- Goal setting: Set clear, achievable goals, create a roadmap for success, and track progress to stay motivated and focused on your objectives.
- Time management: Prioritize tasks, establish routines, and minimize distractions to manage time effectively and maintain focus on important activities.
- Self-care: Prioritize self-care, mental health, and well-being by taking breaks, practicing mindfulness, and engaging in activities that recharge and energize you.
- Accountability: Stay accountable to yourself, set deadlines, seek feedback, and engage with mentors or peers to stay motivated, accountable, and on track toward your goals.

Seeking Support and Mentorship:

Seeking support and mentorship can provide guidance, advice, and encouragement to overcome challenges, stay motivated, and achieve success in online income pursuits. Strategies for seeking support and mentorship include:

- Networking: Build relationships, connect with like-minded individuals, and engage with online communities, forums, and networking groups to seek advice, share experiences, and receive support.
- Mentorship: Find mentors, coaches, or advisors in your industry or field who can provide insights, guidance, and mentorship to help you navigate challenges, make informed decisions, and grow professionally.
- Peer support: Join mastermind groups, accountability partnerships, or peer circles to collaborate, share resources, and receive feedback from peers who can offer support, motivation, and encouragement.
- Online resources: Utilize online resources, courses, webinars, and podcasts to access valuable information, tools, and insights to enhance your skills, knowledge, and motivation in pursuing online income opportunities.

Case Studies:

- Dealing with Setbacks and Failures: Case Study - Entrepreneur Sarah's Resilience Journey

Sarah, an entrepreneur, faces setbacks in her online business due to a product launch failure. Instead of giving up, Sarah reflects on the experience, learns valuable lessons, and pivots her strategy to launch a successful product. Through resilience, adaptability, and persistence, Sarah overcomes setbacks, learns from failures, and achieves success in her online business.

- Maintaining Motivation and Focus: Case Study - Freelancer John's Productivity Habits
John, a freelancer, maintains motivation and focus by setting daily goals, using time-blocking techniques, and practicing self-care. By prioritizing tasks, minimizing distractions, and staying accountable to his schedule, John boosts productivity, sustains motivation, and achieves his online income targets consistently.

- Seeking Support and Mentorship: Case Study - Blogger Emily's Mentorship Success
Emily, a blogger, seeks support and mentorship from an experienced blogger in her niche. Through mentorship, guidance, and feedback, Emily receives valuable insights, strategies, and encouragement to grow her blog, overcome challenges, and stay motivated in her online income journey. By leveraging mentorship, Emily accelerates her growth, gains confidence, and achieves success in her blogging endeavors.

Chapter 14: Legal and Financial Considerations

Tax Implications of Earning Money Online:

Understanding the tax implications of earning money online is crucial for compliance and financial planning. Key aspects of tax implications for online income include:

- Income reporting: Report all online income, including earnings from freelancing, affiliate marketing, e-commerce sales, and other online ventures, on your tax returns.
- Tax deductions: Identify eligible tax deductions for online business expenses such as software, equipment, marketing costs, and home office expenses to reduce taxable income.
- Estimated taxes: Pay estimated taxes quarterly if you expect to owe a certain amount in taxes to avoid penalties and interest for underpayment.
- Tax credits: Explore tax credits, incentives, and deductions available for online businesses, self-employed individuals, and small business owners to maximize tax savings and benefits.

Setting Up a Business Entity:

Setting up a business entity is essential for protecting personal assets, managing liability, and establishing a formal structure for your online business. Considerations for setting up a business entity include:

- Legal structure: Choose a suitable legal structure for your online business, such as a sole proprietorship, partnership, limited liability company (LLC), or corporation, based on your business goals, liability protection needs, and tax considerations.
- Registration: Register your business entity with the appropriate state or local authorities, obtain necessary licenses and permits, and comply with legal requirements to operate your online business legally.
- Business banking: Open a separate business bank account, maintain accurate financial records, and separate personal and business finances to ensure financial transparency, organization, and compliance with tax regulations.
- Contracts and agreements: Draft contracts, terms of service, privacy policies, and other legal documents to protect your business interests, establish clear expectations, and mitigate legal risks in online transactions and relationships.

Protecting Your Online Assets:

Protecting your online assets involves safeguarding intellectual property, data, and digital assets from theft, infringement, or unauthorized use. Strategies for protecting your online assets include:

- Copyrights: Obtain copyrights for original content, designs, images, and creative works to protect intellectual property rights and prevent unauthorized use or reproduction.
- Trademarks: Register trademarks for brand names, logos, and slogans to establish brand identity, prevent brand confusion, and protect your business identity in the marketplace.
- Data security: Implement data security measures, encryption, backups, and secure protocols to protect sensitive information, customer data, and online transactions from cyber threats, hacking, and data breaches.
- Insurance: Consider business insurance policies such as liability insurance, cyber insurance, and professional indemnity insurance to mitigate risks, cover legal expenses, and protect your online assets in case of unforeseen events or disputes.

Case Studies:

- Tax Implications of Earning Money Online: Case Study - Freelancer Sarah's Tax Compliance

Sarah, a freelancer, ensures tax compliance by accurately reporting her online income, tracking business expenses, and filing taxes on time. By consulting with a tax professional, maximizing deductions, and staying informed about tax laws, Sarah manages tax implications effectively, minimizes tax liabilities, and maintains financial transparency in her online income activities.

- Setting Up a Business Entity: Case Study - E-commerce Entrepreneur John's LLC Formation

John, an e-commerce entrepreneur, establishes an LLC for his online business to protect personal assets, limit liability, and formalize his business structure. By registering his LLC, opening a business bank account, and complying with legal requirements, John creates a legal entity that separates personal and business finances, mitigates risks, and provides a framework for growth and expansion.

- Protecting Your Online Assets: Case Study - Blogger Emily's Intellectual Property Protection

Emily, a blogger, protects her online assets by obtaining copyrights for her blog content, trademarks for her brand name, and implementing data security measures to safeguard user data. By securing her intellectual property rights, brand identity, and online data, Emily mitigates risks, defends against infringement, and maintains the integrity and security of her online assets.

Chapter 15: Future Trends in Online Money-Making

Emerging Opportunities in the Digital Space:

Identifying emerging opportunities in the digital space is essential for staying competitive and capitalizing on new trends. Key aspects of emerging opportunities in the digital space include:

- E-commerce innovation: Explore new e-commerce trends such as social commerce, voice commerce, augmented reality shopping, and personalized shopping experiences to enhance customer engagement and drive sales.
- Online services: Tap into growing demand for online services such as virtual events, telemedicine, online education, remote work solutions, and digital entertainment to meet changing consumer needs and preferences.
- Blockchain and cryptocurrency: Embrace blockchain technology, decentralized finance (DeFi), non-fungible tokens (NFTs), and cryptocurrency trends to leverage new financial instruments, investment opportunities, and digital assets in the online economy.
- Sustainability and green tech: Emphasize sustainability, eco-friendly practices, green technologies, and ethical consumerism in online businesses to align with environmental trends, social responsibility, and conscious consumerism.

Adapting to Technological Advancements:

Adapting to technological advancements is crucial for optimizing operations, enhancing user experiences, and staying relevant in the digital landscape. Strategies for adapting to technological advancements include:

- Artificial intelligence: Implement AI-powered tools, chatbots, automation, and machine learning algorithms to streamline processes, personalize interactions, and improve efficiency in online businesses.
- Data analytics: Utilize data analytics, predictive analytics, and business intelligence tools to analyze customer behavior, track performance metrics, and make data-driven decisions for strategic growth and optimization.
- Mobile optimization: Prioritize mobile responsiveness, mobile apps, and mobile-first design to cater to the increasing mobile user base and deliver seamless experiences across devices.
- Internet of Things (IoT): Explore IoT applications, smart devices, connected technologies, and IoT integration to enhance product functionality, gather real-time data, and offer innovative solutions in online products and services.

Staying Ahead in the Online Economy:

Staying ahead in the online economy requires continuous learning, innovation, and adaptability to navigate market shifts and industry disruptions. Strategies for staying ahead in the online economy include:

- Lifelong learning: Invest in continuous education, skills development, and professional growth to stay updated on industry trends, technologies, and best practices in the online economy.
- Innovation mindset: Foster an innovation mindset, embrace creativity, experiment with new ideas, and challenge the status quo to drive innovation, differentiation, and competitive advantage in online ventures.
- Market research: Conduct market research, competitor analysis, and trend forecasting to anticipate consumer needs, identify market gaps, and capitalize on emerging opportunities in the online economy.

- Networking and collaboration: Build strategic partnerships, engage with industry experts, and collaborate with peers to exchange insights, share resources, and stay informed about industry developments and future trends.

Case Studies:

- Emerging Opportunities in the Digital Space: Case Study - Social Commerce Platform Success
A social commerce platform integrates social media features with e-commerce functionalities, enabling users to discover, shop, and transact within social networks. Platforms like Instagram Shopping, Pinterest Shop, and Facebook Marketplace exemplify emerging opportunities in the digital space by blending social engagement with online shopping to create seamless and interactive shopping experiences for users.
- Adapting to Technological Advancements: Case Study - AI-Powered Customer Service Implementation
An e-commerce retailer adopts AI-powered chatbots and customer service automation to enhance customer support, resolve queries, and personalize interactions. By leveraging AI technology, the retailer improves response times, reduces customer service costs, and delivers efficient and personalized customer experiences in line with technological advancements in online customer service.
- Staying Ahead in the Online Economy: Case Study - Digital Marketing Agency Innovation
A digital marketing agency embraces IoT integration, data analytics, and AI tools to optimize digital campaigns, track performance metrics, and deliver targeted marketing strategies for clients. By staying ahead in the online economy through innovation, technology adoption, and strategic partnerships, the agency maintains a competitive edge, drives results for clients, and leads in the dynamic digital marketing landscape.

Appendix

Title: The Ultimate Guide to Earning Money Online

Chapter 1: Introduction to Online Money-Making

- Understanding the digital landscape
- Benefits of earning money online
- Common misconceptions and pitfalls

Chapter 2: Setting the Foundation

- Identifying your skills and interests
- Goal setting and financial planning
- Creating a conducive work environment

Chapter 3: Freelancing

- Overview of freelancing platforms
- Building a strong profile and portfolio
- Finding and securing freelance gigs

Chapter 4: Online Surveys and Market Research

- Participating in paid surveys
- Joining market research panels
- Maximizing earnings from surveys

Chapter 5: E-commerce and Dropshipping

- Setting up an online store
- Dropshipping business model
- Marketing and driving traffic to your store

Chapter 6: Affiliate Marketing

- Understanding affiliate marketing
- Choosing the right affiliate programs
- Strategies for successful affiliate marketing

Chapter 7: Blogging and Content Creation

- Starting a blog
- Monetizing your blog through ads and sponsored content
- Building a loyal audience

Chapter 8: Online Tutoring and Courses

- Offering online tutoring services
- Creating and selling online courses
- Platforms for teaching and learning

Chapter 9: Virtual Assistance and Remote Work

- Providing virtual assistance services
- Finding remote work opportunities
- Managing time and tasks effectively

Chapter 10: Investing and Trading Online

- Introduction to online investing
- Trading stocks, cryptocurrencies, and forex
- Risk management and strategies for success

Chapter 11: Passive Income Streams

- Creating passive income streams online
- Real estate crowdfunding and investments
- Building a portfolio of passive income sources

Chapter 12: Scaling and Diversifying Your Online Income

- Scaling your online business
- Diversifying income streams
- Long-term sustainability and growth

Chapter 13: Overcoming Challenges and Staying Motivated

- Dealing with setbacks and failures
- Maintaining motivation and focus

- Seeking support and mentorship

Chapter 14: Legal and Financial Considerations

- Tax implications of earning money online
- Setting up a business entity
- Protecting your online assets

Chapter 15: Future Trends in Online Money-Making

- Emerging opportunities in the digital space
- Adapting to technological advancements
- Staying ahead in the online economy

This outline provides a structured approach to writing a comprehensive guide on earning money online. Each chapter can be further expanded with practical tips, case studies, and actionable steps to help readers navigate the online landscape and achieve financial success.

www.ingramcontent.com/pod-product-compliance
Lightning Source LLC
Chambersburg PA
CBHW050245230526
45470CB00005B/2126